Halin Garcia-Gordon

Cracking Python

Ace Coding Interviews: Volume 1, Intro to Python

First published by Datasophical 2023

Copyright © 2023 by Halin Garcia-Gordon

All rights reserved. No part of this publication may be reproduced, stored or transmitted in any form or by any means, electronic, mechanical, photocopying, recording, scanning, or otherwise without written permission from the publisher. It is illegal to copy this book, post it to a website, or distribute it by any other means without permission.

This novel is entirely a work of fiction. The names, characters and incidents portrayed in it are the work of the author's imagination. Any resemblance to actual persons, living or dead, events or localities is entirely coincidental.

Designations used by companies to distinguish their products are often claimed as trademarks. All brand names and product names used in this book and on its cover are trade names, service marks, trademarks and registered trademarks of their respective owners. The publishers and the book are not associated with any product or vendor mentioned in this book. None of the companies referenced within the book have endorsed the book.

First edition

Table of Contents

Preface	1
I. LAYING THE GROUNDWORK: THE BASICS OF CODING	3
1. Introduction to Python and Programming Concepts	4
What is Programming?	4
Why Use Python for the Solutions?	8
Installing Python on the Latest Mac and Windows Computers	9
How to Execute Lines of Python One by One	9
What is an IDE and Installing Visual Studio Code	10
Executing Python Files	10
Introduction to LeetCode.com and the Purpose of This Book	10
Coding Challenges and Problems in This Book	11
Our Code Solutions Are on Github, Practice Them	11
Syntax Highlighting in this Book	12
Understanding Camel Case	12
2. Basic Programming Concepts	13
Variables and Data Types	14
The print() Function and Printing Variables	15
Printing Text	16
Printing Variables	16
Debugging	17
Formatted Printing	17
What is an Integer (int)?	18
What is a Float and a Decimal?	18

What is a String (str)?	20
What is a Character (char)?	20
What is a Boolean (bool)?	21

3. Control Structures — 22

Conditional Statements (If, Elif, and Else)	23
Spacing and indentation Indentation in 'If' Statements	24
What are Python operators like `==`, `!=`, and `<=`?	24
Loops	25
For Loops	25
While Loops	27

4. Functions — 28

What is a Function?	29
Self, Class, and Instances in Python	30
Spacing and Indentation in Function Declarations	31
The `return` Keyword	32
String Functions and String Slicing	32
More Built-in Functions: max() and min()	33

5. Data Structures — 35

Lists	36
Sets	37
Dictionaries	38
Other Data Structures	39

6. Introduction to Algorithms — 40

What are Algorithms?	41
Sorting Algorithms	41
Searching Algorithms	41

7. Introduction to Big-O Notation — 43

O(1) - Constant Time Complexity	44

O(n) - Linear Time Complexity	44
O(NK) - Linear Time Complexity with a Constant Factor	44
O(log n) - Logarithmic Time Complexity	45
O(n*log n) - Linearithmic Time Complexity	45
O(k*log n) - Linearithmic Time Complexity with a Constant Factor	46
O(n^2) - Quadratic Time Complexity	47
Big-O Notation Summary	51
A Big-O Real-world Scenario	51
A Big-O Interview Question	52
Comparing Big-O Time Complexities using Graphs	53
II. ENGAGING STORIES, CODE, AND INTERVIEW SOLUTIONS	**56**
8. The Exclusive Music Festival	57
About the Author	61

Preface

In your hands, you hold more than just a book – it's the first step on a journey of discovery. The goal of this book series is to provide specific guidance and instruction that enables you to secure employment at prestigious technology companies such as Google, Apple, Facebook (now Meta), Microsoft, as well as fast-growing startups and many others. This is the first volume in a comprehensive series, this guide serves as your catalyst for growth, a roadmap to mastering software engineering, and a mentor guiding you through the intricate labyrinth of technology. This book reflects years of professional experience, countless hours of tireless effort, and my unwavering dedication to helping you unlock your full potential in the realm of software engineering.

This series is designed to be your companion, a source of knowledge that you can refer to time and again. Each chapter builds on the last, layering complex concepts with practical examples, metaphors, and stories to make these concepts easier to understand and remember. However, your learning journey doesn't have to be linear. Feel free to jump to sections that pique your interest or tackle areas where you feel you need more practice.

Throughout your journey, remember that understanding takes time. Patience, persistence, and practice are your best allies. Take your time with each concept, and don't be afraid to revisit previous sections for clarity. Moreover, make sure you frequently practice and experiment with the code solutions to the interview problems in this book, they can be found here:
https://github.com/Datasophical/CrackingPythonVol1

Your feedback is invaluable in making this book a better resource for everyone. If you have suggestions, questions, or comments, I encourage you to reach out to me directly at ceo@datasophical.com. Your insights and experiences will help improve future editions.

Moreover, if you find this book helpful, please consider leaving a review on Amazon. Your reviews not only help others discover this resource, but they also provide me with invaluable feedback on how well the book is serving its purpose.

Thank you for embarking on this journey with me. I look forward to hearing about your progress, challenges, triumphs, and, most importantly, your growth. Here's to your success in mastering the art of software engineering!

Ready to code your future? Let's get started!

-Halin Garcia-Gordon

Part I

Laying the Groundwork: The Basics of Coding

In this introductory section, we will begin by covering the fundamental principles of coding. This foundation is vital, as it forms the bedrock upon which all further learning will be built. Remember, every expert was once a beginner. As you embark on this journey, keep an open mind, embrace challenges, and remember that every step forward, no matter how small, is progress. So, let's get started. The road to a fulfilling career in technology starts here.

Chapter 1

Introduction to Python and Programming Concepts

The goal of this book is to provide specific guidance and instruction to enable individuals to secure employment at some of the most prestigious technology companies, such as Google, Apple, Facebook (now Meta), Microsoft, startup companies, and many others. This book, as well as the future series, is designed to prepare you for the most challenging aspects of technical interviews across various roles. These roles include but are not limited to, Software Engineer, Security Engineer, and Data Engineer, along with many other engineering positions that involve coding.

What is Programming?

Programming is the process of creating a set of instructions that tell a computer how to perform a task, just like a recipe. It's like baking a cake, but the ingredients are logic and algorithms, and the oven is your computer that processes these to create a functioning software or application.

Logic and algorithms are like ingredients:

Logic and algorithms are also like cooking tools:

Your computer is like an oven:

Websites, software, and apps are like a baked cake:

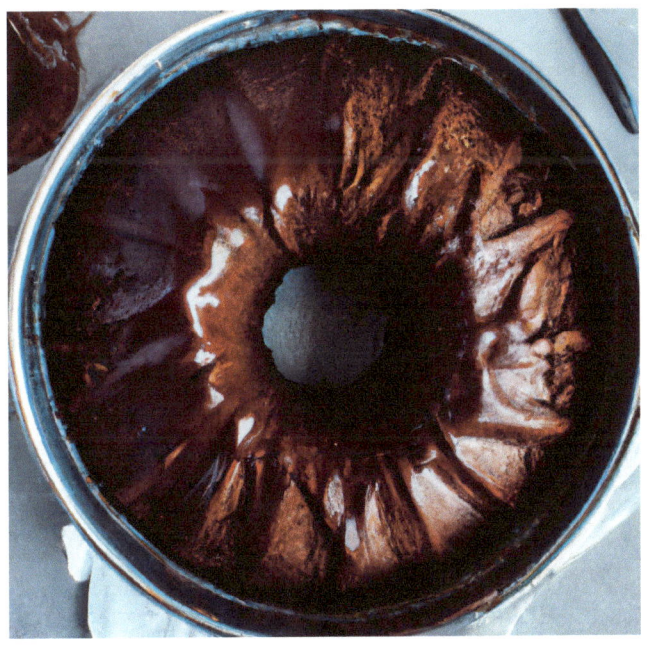

Why Use Python for the Solutions?

Python is a popular programming language known for its simplicity and readability, making it an ideal choice for beginners. It is versatile and powerful, used in various fields such as data analysis, web development, artificial intelligence, and more. Python is used in this book because its syntax is clear and easy to understand, great for explaining complex programming concepts.

Installing Python on the Latest Mac and Windows Computers

We will be using Python 3 as the version for this book. Python 3 can be downloaded from the official Python website (https://www.python.org/), where you can find versions for both Mac and Windows. Follow the instructions for your specific operating system, and remember to verify your installation by checking the Python version in your system's command line or terminal. Don't worry about the exact version of Python 3, the latest should be fine if it's Python 3.

How to Execute Lines of Python One by One

To execute lines of Python one by one, you can use the Python interactive shell within your command line or terminal on your computer. Integrated Development Environments (IDEs) also come with this feature. Enter your code line by line, and the shell or IDE will run your code, providing immediate feedback.

> Here is an example on Mac using the "Terminal" app, which is pre-installed:

What is an IDE and Installing Visual Studio Code

An Integrated Development Environment (IDE) is a software application that provides a comprehensive set of tools for software development. Visual Studio Code (VS Code) is one such IDE that is free, open-source, and supports a variety of programming languages, including Python. You can download VS Code from the official website (https://code.visualstudio.com/) and follow the instructions to install it on your system.

Executing Python Files

Once you've written your Python code in a file with a .py extension, you can run it using Python's interpreter in the command line or terminal. Navigate to the directory containing your Python file and type `python3 filename.py` to execute the program. Note that "filename" is whatever you named your file and it can be named anything.

Introduction to LeetCode.com and the Purpose of This Book

LeetCode.com is an online platform that offers a comprehensive collection of coding challenges designed to help you prepare for technical job interviews. Top technology companies like Google, Apple, Facebook (now Meta), Microsoft, and others often ask interview questions that are similar to, or in some cases, identical to those found on LeetCode.com. Their platform allows you to write and test your code directly on their site, using their online compiler to check your solutions. The problems discussed and analyzed in this book are inspired by the types of challenges that you would encounter on LeetCode.com. All content on the Leetcode.com site is Leetcode's sole and exclusive property and Datasophical is a separate entity.

Coding Challenges and Problems in This Book

This book includes discussions and analyses of a variety of coding problems inspired by the challenges found on LeetCode.com. Each problem in this book is not only a lesson but a story. We use real-life scenarios to illustrate when and how these coding solutions can be applied, making them more relatable and easier to remember. Moreover, our careful choice of variable names and clear explanations aid in simplifying the complexities, leading to better comprehension and a more enjoyable experience than your average textbook! While we'll delve into these problems in detail, we strongly encourage you to visit LeetCode.com for the full problem statements. Testing your solutions using LeetCode's online compiler will not only provide you with instant feedback but also familiarize you with the platform's environment, further enhancing your interview preparation. **To run our code on the Leetcode.com website, don't forget to change our class names to "Class Solution." For example: "Class PalindromeRapper" should become "Class Solution", or your code will throw an error. You may also need to change the function name from our function name to the Leetcode function name. You can also run your code locally on your computer with your installed version of Python 3.**

Our Code Solutions Are on Github, Practice Them

One of the best ways to get better at coding is to practice coding. Try experimenting with our code solutions by changing certain details or printing out variables. By running our code on your local computer, you can better understand the flow of each code solution. You can find our code solutions on Github.com through this link:
https://github.com/Datasophical/CrackingPythonVol1

Syntax Highlighting in this Book

In this book, you'll notice that Python code is written in different colors. This is known as syntax highlighting, a feature that displays text, especially source code, in different colors and fonts according to the category of terms.

Syntax, in the context of programming, refers to the set of rules that defines the combinations of symbols considered correctly structured in a particular programming language. It's the way commands are structured and how they must be written to be properly understood and executed by a computer. Syntax includes rules about where to place certain keywords, how to structure functions and loops, and how to organize code in a way that the computer can interpret correctly.

Syntax highlighting is a feature used in text editors and integrated development environments (IDEs) that changes the color of different parts of the code to make it more readable. For example, function names might be one color, variables another, and strings a third color, don't worry about what these examples of syntax mean, we will explain in a couple of sections. This color coding makes it easier to understand the structure of the code at a glance. It can also help you spot errors, for example, if something is highlighted red or it's the wrong color, it might be because you've violated a syntax rule.

By using syntax highlighting in this book, we aim to make the code examples more understandable and easier to follow, aiding your learning process.

Understanding Camel Case

Camel case is a practice in programming where the first letter of each variable name is made lowercase and the middle of a variable name is capitalized to make it more readable. For example, `weightMap` uses camel case. This is just one of several casing conventions, and it's a frequently used style in Python. It is not required but encouraged.

Chapter 2

Basic Programming Concepts

As you embark on your programming journey, it's important to become familiar with certain fundamental concepts. These concepts form the backbone of almost every program you'll write. In this section, we'll explore these basic programming concepts in the context of Python, one of the most intuitive and widely used programming languages today.

Variables and Data Types

In programming, a variable is a named space in the computer's memory where a programmer can store data and later retrieve that data using the variable's name. Data types define the kind of data that can be stored in a variable. Python, like other programming languages, supports several different types of data. Let's explore a few of these.

The print() Function and Printing Variables

In Python, the `print()` function is used to output information to the console, which is a text-based user interface that allows interaction with the program by displaying output and receiving input. You can print text, variables, or the results of expressions.

Printing Text

To print simple text (also known as a string), you can pass the text you want to print to the `print()` function, enclosed in either single or double quotes. Here's an example:

```
print("Hello, World!")
```

When you run this program, it will output:

Hello, World!

Printing Variables

A variable in Python is a name that you assign to a piece of data. For example, you might assign the number 10 to a variable called `my_number`:

```
my_number = 10
```

You can print the value of a variable using the `print()` function. Just pass the name of the variable to the function:

```
print(my_number)
```

This will output:

10

Debugging

Debugging is the process of fixing errors and identifying issues in your code. Using `print()` is one of the simplest methods to see what's going on inside your program. When you're writing complex programs, it's not always immediately clear what each part of your code is doing. By strategically placing `print()` statements throughout your code, you can monitor the values of your variables at different points in your program's execution, and this can help you find where things might be going wrong.

Formatted Printing

Python also offers several ways to format your output. One of the most common ways is using f-strings (formatted string literals). They are prefixed with 'f' and are enclosed by quotes. Variables can be referenced inside an f-string using curly braces `{}`. Here's an example:

```python
name = "Alice"
age = 12
print(f"Hello, {name}. You are {age} years old.")
```

This will output:

Hello, Alice. You are 12 years old.

What is an Integer (int)?

An int, short for integer, is a numerical data type that can represent whole numbers, both positive and negative, but without a decimal point. Examples of integers are 7, -3, and 100. They are typically used when you're counting things or when the numbers you're working with don't require fractional values. An example:

```
int_example = 7

print(f"The variable 'int_example' holds the integer value {int_example} and its type is {type(int_example)}.")
```

Note: The `print` statement is on one line.

When you run this, you'll see that `int_example` is an integer and its value is 7.

What is a Float and a Decimal?

A float, short for floating point number, is a numerical data type that can represent real numbers, both large and small, with decimal points. For example, numbers like 3.14, 0.01, and -27.89 are floats. They are useful when you need more precision in calculations than integers can provide. An example:

```
float_example = 3.14

print(f"The variable 'float_example' holds the floating point value {float_example} and its type is {type(float_example)}.")
```

Running the above shows that `float_example` is a float and its value is 3.14.

It's important to note there are potential pitfalls when using Python's built-in `float` type for financial calculations involving real money. The primary issue lies in the precision of floating-point arithmetic.

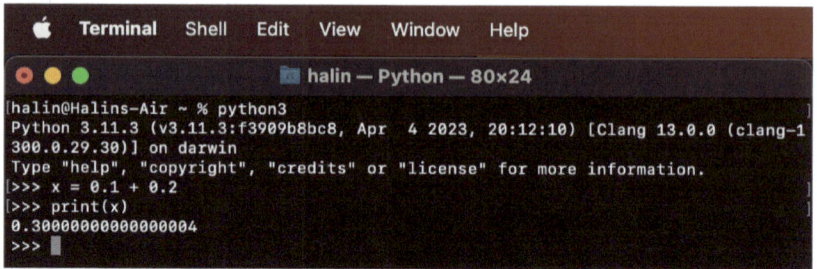

1. **Precision**: Floating-point numbers in Python (and in most other programming languages) use binary floating-point representation, which can lead to precision issues. For example, a simple operation like `0.1 + 0.2` doesn't result in `0.3` as expected, but rather a slightly different number due to the way floating-point numbers are represented in binary.
2. **Rounding Errors**: These precision issues can lead to rounding errors when performing mathematical operations. This is especially problematic in financial applications where precise calculations and comparisons are vital.

To overcome these issues, Python has a `decimal` module for decimal fixed point and floating point arithmetic. It provides decimal floating point numbers which are represented exactly up to a fixed number of digits, which can be specified. This can be more accurate for financial calculations. Another alternative is to use integer arithmetic, where all money amounts are represented as multiples of the smallest currency unit (for example, cents in the case of dollars).

What is a String (str)?

A string, also abbreviated as "str", is a sequence of one or more characters that could include letters, numbers, whitespace characters (like a space or a tab), or any other symbols. In Python, you create a string by enclosing characters in either single quotes (' '), double quotes (" "), or triple quotes (''' ''' or """ """). Strings are used when you're working with text. For example, "Hello, World!" and "Python is legit!" are both strings. An example:

```
string_example = "Hello, World!"
print(f"The variable 'string_example' holds the string value '{string_example}' and its type is {type(string_example)}.")
```

Running this will show that `string_example` is a string and its value is "Hello, World!".

What is a Character (char)?

A character, also referred to as a "char", in programming generally refers to any single textual unit, including letters (like 'a', 'B'), digits (like '2', '9'), punctuation marks (like '!', ','), and even whitespace (' '). In Python, a character is just a string of length one. For example, 'a' and '7' are both characters but their type would resolve to 'str.' An example:

```
char_example = 'a'
print(f"The variable 'char_example' holds the character value '{char_example}' and its type is {type(char_example)}.")
```

Running this code shows that `char_example` is represented as a string in Python and its value is 'a'.

What is a Boolean (bool)?

A boolean, or `bool`, is a type of data in Python that can only be one of two values: `True` or `False`. You can think of it as a switch that can be either **on** (`True`) or **off** (`False`). Booleans are used in programming when you need to check if a certain condition is true or not. Here's a simple example of how booleans can be used in Python:

```
is_sunny = True

if is_sunny:
    print("Let's go outside!")
else:
    print("Better stay indoors.")
```

In this example, `is_sunny` is a Boolean variable that is set to `True`. The `if` statement checks if `is_sunny` is `True`. If it is, the message "Let's go outside!" is printed. If `is_sunny` were `False`, the message "Better stay indoors." would be printed instead.

You'll find that booleans are incredibly useful in controlling the flow of your programs. They are often used in conditional statements, loops, and comparisons. We will explain these in the next couple of sections.

Chapter 3

Control Structures

Control structures guide the flow of your program and the choices your program makes. They decide what code gets executed and when, making them an essential part of any programming language. Here are some of the most common control structures used in Python:

Conditional Statements (If, Elif, and Else)

Conditional statements allow your program to make decisions. In Python, you can use `if`, `elif`, and `else` to control which parts of your code run based on whether certain conditions are met. Here's a simple example:

```
weather = "sunny"

if weather == "sunny":
    print("Let's go outside!")
elif weather == "rainy":
    print("Better stay indoors.")
else:
    print("Check the weather again.")
```

In this example, if `weather` is "sunny", the program will print "Let's go outside!". If `weather` is "rainy", it will print "Better stay indoors.". For any other value of `weather`, it will print "Check the weather again."

Here is an overview of each conditional keyword:

1. **if**: This is the initial condition check. Python will execute the code inside the `if` block if the condition is **True**.
2. **elif** (which stands for "else if"): This lets you check for additional conditions if the first `if` condition isn't met. Python will move on to the `elif` condition if the `if` condition was **False**.
3. **else**: This is a catch-all for any conditions not caught by the `if` and `elif` statements. If all previous conditions are **False**, Python will execute the code inside the `else` block. You can think of it as the default action if no other conditions are met.

Spacing and indentation Indentation in 'If' Statements

In Python, indentation (spaces at the start of a line) forms a 'block' of code. Think of it as a group of instructions working together when called upon. Without proper indentation, Python gets confused about which lines of code belong to the group.

When we create an `if` statement, we need to indent the following lines of code that are part of this `if` statement. **This can be done using 4 spaces or a tab.** It's like saying to Python, 'Hey, these indented lines are under my command!' Once we stop indenting, Python gets the message that we're done with this `if` statement.

What are Python operators like `==`, `!=`, and `<=`?

These operators in Python, such as `==`, `<=`, `<`, and `!=`, play a crucial role in forming conditions, comparisons, and Boolean operations.

The `==` operator checks if the value on its left is equal to the value on its right. For example, `7 == 7` is `True` because both sides are equal, while `7 == 8` is `False` because the two sides are not equal.

The `<` operator, or "less than", checks if the value on its left is less than and not equal to the value on its right. For example, `3 < 4` is `True` because 3 is less than 4, but `5 < 5` is `False` because 5 is not less than itself.

The `<=` operator, standing for "less than or equal to", is like a combination of the first two examples, it checks if the value on its left is either less than or equal to the value on its right. For example, `4 <= 5` is `True` because 4 is indeed less than 5, and `6 <= 6` is also `True` because 6 equals 6.

Lastly, the `!=` operator, standing for "not equal to", verifies that the value on its left is not equal to the value on its right. `9 != 10` is `True` because 9 is not equal to 10, while `10 != 10` is `False` because both sides are equal.

These operators are the building blocks for controlling the flow of your program because they allow your code to make decisions and react differently depending on the specific conditions at hand.

Loops

Loops allow you to repeat a block of code multiple times. This is especially useful when you want to operate on each item in a list or when you want to repeat a task until a certain condition is met.

In Python, you have <u>two types of loops</u>: `for` and `while`.

For Loops

You know how in school when your teacher asks you to go through each question on your homework and check your answers? You start from the first question, then move to the second question, then the third, and so on until you reach the end. That process of going through each question one by one is a lot like what we mean when we say a computer "**iterates**".

In computer science, when we say a program "iterates" over something like a list or a collection of items, it means it's going through each item one by one, just like you did with your homework questions. It starts from the first item, does something with it (like checks if it's the answer we're looking for), then moves on to the next item, and the next, until it has gone through all the items.

So, in a nutshell, "to iterate" in computer science is like the computer's way of checking its homework!

A `for` loop in Python iterates over a sequence, a list, a string, or any other iterable object. Here's an example:

```
for i in range(5):
    print(i)
```

The output (in other words, the result) of this code is:

0

1

2

3

4

Running this code prints the numbers 0 through 4. The function `range(5)` generates a sequence of numbers starting from 0 and ending at 4. The `for` loop then steps in and iterates over this sequence, which means it goes through each number one by one. As it visits each number, it uses the variable `i` to hold that number temporarily, and then it prints `i`. Think of `i` as a placeholder that takes on the value of each number in the sequence as the `for` loop makes its way through. In this context, `range()` is the function that creates our sequence, and `5` is the input we give to `range()` to tell it how many numbers we want in our sequence.

While Loops

A `while` loop in Python repeats a block of code as long as a certain condition is **True**. Here's an example:

```
counter = 0

while counter < 5:
    print(counter)
    counter += 1
```

In this example, as long as `counter` is less than 5, the program will print `counter` and then increase `counter` by 1. In Python, `counter += 1` is a shorter, but just as powerful, way to write `counter = counter + 1`

Remember, control structures are crucial for guiding the flow of your program. As you continue your journey in Python, you'll find these structures to be fundamental building blocks in creating complex and dynamic programs.

Chapter 4

Functions

Imagine you're the director of a big event, say, a prom or a concert. To manage such a large event, you would divide the tasks and delegate them to different teams or committees, right? Similarly, in the world of programming, we divide a large problem into smaller, manageable tasks. Each of these tasks is handled by a **function**.

What is a Function?

A **function**, sometimes referred to as a **method**, is essentially a self-contained piece of code within a larger program. By keeping functions short and specific in Python programming, you create neat and efficient blocks of code. These blocks not only enhance the cleanliness and organization of your code but also make it easier to read and enable code reuse. This can save you a lot of time and effort!

In Python, we define a function using the keyword `def`, which stands for "define". After `def`, we give the function a name and then parentheses `()`. Inside these parentheses, we can list **parameters**, which are the special inputs the function uses to do its job, you can think of parameters as the special ingredients that a function needs to do its work. After the parentheses, we need a colon `:` and then we start the body of the function on the next line. The body is where the function does its work. Let's look at an example to understand this better:

```
def checkQRcodes(self, guests: List[int]) -> bool:
    # code to check QR codes goes here
```

Note: In Python, any line starting with `#` is a comment and will be ignored and not run.

In this function, `checkQRcodes` is the name of the function, and `guests` is a parameter. This function is supposed to check the QR codes of the guests.

Now, you might have noticed that the `guests` parameter has `List[int]` next to it. This is a feature of Python 3 called **type hinting**. Type hinting is a way for programmers to indicate the expected type of a function's inputs or its expected return type, please note that type hinting is completely optional but makes your code more clear. For example:
`def checkQRcodes(self, guests):`
... would be just as valid. `List[int]` tells us that `guests` should be a list of integers and the function should return a boolean type variable which would either be **True** or **False**.

Self, Class, and Instances in Python

In Python programming, think of a `class` as a blueprint or a set of instructions for creating something, while an 'instance' is the actual thing you create using that blueprint. For example, if the `class` is like a recipe for a cake, an 'instance' would be the actual cake you bake following that recipe.

Now, `self` in Python is a way to refer to these individual 'cakes' or instances that we create. When used inside a function within a class, `self` helps that function know which exact 'cake' (or instance) it needs to work with. It does this by being the first parameter in the function.

So when you see `self` in Python, just think of it as a placeholder for the specific instance of the class that you're dealing with at any given moment. This helps the function know which specific instance it's working with and allows it to use the class's attributes and other functions. Let's take a look at our example:

```python
def checkQRcodes(self, guests: List[int]) -> bool:
    # code to check QR codes goes here
```

In this context, `checkQRcodes` is an instance function of some class (which isn't shown in the example). `self` is the first parameter, and it refers to the instance of the class on which `checkQRcodes` is being called. This allows `checkQRcodes` to access and modify other attributes or functions within the same instance. Here's a more complete example to illustrate this:

```python
class Event:
    def __init__(self):
        self.guests = []

    def add_guest(self, guest_id: int):
        self.guests.append(guest_id)

    def checkQRcodes(self, guests: List[int]) -> bool:
        for guest in guests:
            if guest not in self.guests:
                return False
        return True
```

In this example, an `Event` class is defined with an instance function `checkQRcodes`. `self` is used to access the `guests` attribute of the instance. So when `checkQRcodes` is called on an instance of `Event`, it can check against the `guests` of that specific instance.

Spacing and Indentation in Function Declarations

When we define a function using **def**, the subsequent lines of code that belong to this function **must be indented by 4 spaces or a tab.** This makes it clear to Python that these instructions are part of the function. Once we end the indentation, Python knows that we've finished defining the function.

The `return` Keyword

When a function completes its task, it can "give" something back to the line of code that called it. This is done using the `return` keyword. `return` sends a result back to the caller and <u>also serves as a way to exit the function.</u>

For instance, if our `checkQRcodes` function is supposed to tell us if all the QR codes are valid, it could give us a `True` or `False` result. We could write it like this:

```python
def checkQRcodes(guests):
    # code to check QR codes goes here
    # let's say we store the result in a variable called 'all_valid'
    return all_valid
```

In this version of the function, `return all_valid` means that the function will give back the value of `all_valid` when it's called. If `all_valid` is `True`, that means all the QR codes were valid. If `all_valid` is `False`, that means at least one QR code was invalid.

The `return` keyword isn't required in a function, but it's very useful when you want the function to produce a result that you can use elsewhere in your code.

String Functions and String Slicing

Python provides a set of built-in functions (also called methods) that help you manipulate strings. For instance, the `lower()` function converts all the characters in a string to lowercase. This can be useful in a variety of scenarios, such as ignoring case when comparing two strings, for example:
`heLLo == hello` would return `False`
`heLLo.lower() == hello` would return `True`

Here's an example of using `lower()` in a function:

```python
def is_palindrome(word):
    # Convert the word to lowercase
    word = word.lower()

    # Reverse the word and compare it to the original
    return word == word[::-1]
```

Note: In Python, any line starting with # is a comment and will be ignored and not run.

In the `is_palindrome` function, `word.lower()` converts the input word to lowercase, so the function works even if the input word has capital letters. The function then checks if the word is the same when reversed, which is the condition for being a palindrome. In Python, `word[::-1]` is a handy way to reverse a string. This uses the **slicing** feature in Python, which works on strings and lists.

Let's break it down:
- The first colon `:` means start at the beginning.
- The second colon `:` means go all the way to the end.
- The `-1` tells Python to step backward by one through the word.

So, `word[::-1]` essentially means "start at the beginning, go all the way to the end, but step backward," which is how Python reverses a string or a list. Imagine you've got a `word`, let's say 'HELLO', so `word[::-1]` would turn `word` into 'OLLEH', so we get every letter in reverse order!

More Built-in Functions: max() and min()

Python comes equipped with many more built-in functions that can make your life as a programmer easier. Two such functions are `**max()**` and `**min()**`.

The `max` function returns the largest item in an iterable (like a list) or the largest of two or more arguments. Here's an example:

```
numbers = [3, 5, 2, 8, 6]
print(max(numbers))    # Output: 8
```

In this case, `max` is looking at all the items in the list `numbers` and returning the largest one, which is 8.

Similarly, the `min` function returns the smallest item in an iterable or the smallest of two or more arguments.

For instance:

```
print(min(numbers))    # Output: 2
```

Here, `min` is finding the smallest item in the list `numbers`, which is 2.

These functions can be extremely handy when you're working with lists of numbers and you need to quickly find the largest or smallest number. But remember, they can work with other data types too, as long as it makes sense to find a 'maximum' or 'minimum' of that data type. For example, when used with strings, `max` and `min` can be used to find the string that would come last or first in alphabetical order.

Chapter 5

Data Structures

Now that you've got a good grip on the basics, it's time to dive into something a little more complex but incredibly useful: data structures. Data structures are containers that hold data and have specific functions for accessing and manipulating that data. In Python, one of the most commonly used data structures is the list.

Lists

A Python list is a collection of items that are ordered and changeable. It allows duplicate members, meaning you can have the same item more than once in a list. Lists are great for storing items that belong together.

Let's imagine we're organizing a party. We might have a list of guests like this:

```
guests = ['Alice', 'Bob', 'Charlie', 'Dave']
```

In this example, `guests` is a list that contains four items, each of which is a string. Lists are surrounded by square brackets `[]`, and the items inside the list are separated by commas.

One of the great things about lists in Python is that they can hold any type of data. So, while our `guests` list holds strings, we could have a list that holds integers:

```
ages = [12, 15, 14, 16]
```

Or even a list that holds other lists (we call these 'nested' lists):

```
party = [['Alice', 12], ['Bob', 15], ['Charlie', 14], ['Dave', 16]]
```

Here are some examples of accessing the above `party` list:

`party[0]` would return `['Alice', 12]`

`party[0][0]` would return **'Alice'**

In the `party` list, each item is a smaller list that contains a name and an age.

One of the first things to grasp when working with lists is how to access individual items. Each item in a Python list is assigned a distinct position, or index, that you can use to access it. The indexing in Python lists starts from zero, which might seem unusual if you're new to programming. This means that the first item in the list is at index 0, the second item is at index 1, and so on. It's important to try practicing this on your computer, try playing with the index numbers of `party`.

Using the `guests` list from the previous example:

```
guests = ['Alice', 'Bob', 'Charlie', 'Dave']
```

You would access the first guest, 'Alice', like this:

```
first_guest = guests[0]
```

And the third guest, 'Charlie', like this:

```
third_guest = guests[2]
```

There are lots of operations you can perform on lists, such as adding items, removing items, modifying elements, and slicing or sorting the list. We'll get into more detail about those operations as we go along. For now, just remember that a list is a collection of items, and it's one of the most useful tools Python gives you for organizing your data.

Sets

Let's take a look at another useful data structure in Python: the set. A set is an unordered collection of items where every item is unique (in other words, no duplicate items are allowed). This is similar to how sets work in mathematics.

Here's an example of a set in Python:

```
fruits = {'apple', 'banana', 'cherry', 'apple'}
```

Even though we tried to add 'apple' twice, when we print the set, we'll see that 'apple' only appears once, because **sets do not store duplicates**:

```
print(fruits)    # Output: {'cherry', 'banana', 'apple'}
```

Sets are great when you want to keep track of a collection of unique elements, but you don't care about their order, you don't have duplicates (they are not allowed in sets), and you don't need to access them by an index or a key. However, because a set is an iterable, you can still go through the elements of a set using a `for` loop, but they may not print in the order that you expect, the order in which you access the elements may not be the order in which they were added to the set.

Dictionaries

Next up is the dictionary, often just called a dict. Dictionaries are incredibly useful and versatile data structures in Python. A dictionary is a collection of items that are stored as key:value pairs. The key is used to identify the item and must be unique to the dictionary (**no duplicate keys**). The value holds the data and can be of any type. Here's an example:

```
student = {'name': 'Alice', 'age': 14, 'grade': 8}
```

In this dictionary, there are three elements:

1. 'name' is a key and `Alice` is its value.
2. 'age' is a key and 14 is its value.
3. 'grade' is a key and 8 is its value.

Dictionaries are really good when you need a logical association between a key:value pair. When you have a lot of data that you want to keep track of, and you need to look it up quickly, dictionaries can be a great tool.

Other Data Structures

There are other data structures in Python, like tuples and custom classes, but we'll start with these three: lists, sets, and dictionaries. As you get more comfortable with Python, you'll start to see when it's best to use one data structure over another, this is a key skill to have that coding interviews will test you on. The most important thing is to understand the basic concept: data structures help you organize and manipulate your data, making it easier for you to write effective and efficient code.

Chapter 6

Introduction to Algorithms

What are Algorithms?

Algorithms are like the secret recipes of programming. They're step-by-step instructions that tell a computer exactly what to do to solve a particular problem. Just like how a recipe tells you how to turn a bunch of ingredients into a delicious cake, an algorithm tells a computer how to turn input data into the output or result you want.

To start our journey into the world of algorithms, we're going to look at two types of algorithms that are fundamental to computer science: sorting and searching algorithms.

Sorting Algorithms

Let's imagine you're a music producer and you recorded tracks for an album. The tracks are currently in a random order, and you need to arrange them so that they flow well and provide the best listening experience. This is what a sorting algorithm does: it takes a list of items and arranges them in a specific order.

There are many different sorting algorithms, and each one has its strengths and weaknesses. Some popular examples include bubble sort, insertion sort, and quicksort. We'll take a closer look at these in later, more advanced volumes. **More books will be released soon!**

Searching Algorithms

Now, imagine you're a detective trying to find a missing dog in a big city. Where do you start? How do you decide where to look next? This is the kind of problem a searching algorithm solves: it finds a specific item in a list or a more complex structure like a graph or a tree.

Like with sorting, there are many different searching algorithms, such as linear search and binary search. The right algorithm to use depends on the specific problem you're trying to solve. In a coding interview, the interviewer often provides additional details on the problem they present. These details may hint at one algorithm being a better solution than others. So ask lots of questions! Interviewers will be impressed by insightful questions.

In the following chapters, we'll delve into the science of comparing algorithms. Just like the interviewers will do, we will also focus on comparing the time speeds and memory efficiency of different algorithms.

Chapter 7

Introduction to Big-O Notation

As we delve deeper into the world of algorithms, it becomes crucial to understand how to measure their efficiency. This is where Big-O notation comes in. It's like a speedometer for our algorithms, telling us how fast they can run or how much memory they use, <u>as the amount of data they have to work with increases.</u>

Let's dive into some common Big-O notations:

O(1) - Constant Time Complexity

Imagine you're taking a mirror selfie. No matter how many other photos you have on your phone, taking one more selfie always requires the same amount of effort: you have to pose, snap the picture, and maybe apply a filter or two. It doesn't get any harder if you already have a hundred or a thousand photos on your phone.

This is what we call O(1), or constant time complexity. No matter how big the input is (in this case, the number of photos on your phone), it always takes the same amount of time (or space) to take a new selfie.

O(n) - Linear Time Complexity

Now, suppose you have a playlist of songs written on a piece of paper, and you need to find a specific song by looking at each song one by one. As the number of songs in your playlist increases, the time it takes to find the song also increases at the same rate. This is O(n) time complexity, where n represents the size of your playlist.

O(NK) - Linear Time Complexity with a Constant Factor

Now, let's imagine you want to organize a photoshoot with your friends. You want to take a group picture for each possible combination of friends. If you have N friends, and you want to take photos in groups of K, then the amount of work you have to do increases as the number of friends and the group size increases.

This is an example of O(NK) time complexity, which could also be written as O(n*k). The time or space required grows with the size of the input (N) and another factor (K).

O(log n) - Logarithmic Time Complexity

Imagine you're trying to guess a number between 1 and 100, and every time you make a guess, a friend tells you if your guess is too high or too low. You can use this information to rule out half of the remaining numbers each time, which greatly speeds up your search. This is an example of O(log n) time complexity, which can also be written as O(log(n)) or O(logn). It is much faster than O(n), especially when n is large.

O(n*log n) - Linearithmic Time Complexity

Imagine you're organizing a big school party, and you're making a guest list. Each time you add a new guest, you want to keep the list sorted alphabetically.

Now, think of this process as a small project. The complexity of this project doesn't increase very quickly with each new guest. It's more like counting the number of times you have to double 1 (1, 2, 4, 8, etc.) until you reach your guest count. For example, if you have 8 guests, you only need three steps to double 1 to get to 8 (1 becomes 2, 2 becomes 4, 4 becomes 8). So even though you have 8 guests, the 'doubling steps' or 'logarithmic steps' are only 3. This slow growth in steps, no matter how big the guest list gets, is what we call 'logarithmic growth', or O(log n).

But if you're adding 'n' guests, you're essentially doing this small project 'n' times. So the overall 'complexity' of adding n guests and keeping the list sorted becomes O(n*log n). This might seem complicated, but it just means for each new guest you add, you're doing a little project where the complexity grows slowly. So, whether you see it written as O(n*log n), O(nlog n), O(nlogn), or O(n log n), they all mean the same thing.

O(k*log n) - Linearithmic Time Complexity with a Constant Factor

Imagine you're organizing a big music festival with many stages. You need to bring a certain number of artists on each stage, let's call this number 'n'. To ensure the best line-up, you want to keep the schedule for the artists sorted by popularity.

Every time you add an artist and sort the schedule list, it's like doing a small project. The complexity of this project doesn't increase very fast when adding each new artist. It's more like counting the number of times you have to double 1 until you reach the total number of artists 'n' on the stage. For example, if you need to have 8 artists, you only need to double 1 three times (1 becomes 2, 2 becomes 4, 4 becomes 8). So even though you have 8 artists, the 'doubling steps' or 'logarithmic steps' is only 3. This slow growth in steps, no matter how big the artist list gets, is what we call 'logarithmic growth', or O(log n).

Now, let's say you have 'k' stages. This means you'll be doing this small project 'k' times. So the overall 'complexity' of sorting n artists on k stages becomes O(k*log n). This just means for each stage with 'n' artists, you're doing a little project where the complexity grows slowly, like counting the doubling steps instead of counting the actual artist count. So, whether you see it written as O(k*log n), O(k log n), or any other similar notation, they all mean the same thing.

O(n²) - Quadratic Time Complexity

Imagine you're in a class with n students, and you want to find out if any two students have the same birthday. You could compare each student's birthday with every other student's birthday. As the number of students increases, the time it takes to find an answer grows quadratically. This is $O(n^2)$ complexity. Here's a code example of this:

```python
def has_duplicate_birthdays(students):
    n = len(students)
    for i in range(n):
        for j in range(i + 1, n):
            if students[i] == students[j]:
                return True
    return False
```

In this function, the `students` list contains the birthdays of each student in the class. The function works by comparing each student's birthday with every other student's birthday. If it finds a pair of students with the same birthday, it returns `True`. If it goes through all pairs without finding a match, it returns `False`. Note that `len(students)` returns the total number of students in the class. Also, let's review the `range()` function:

The `range()` function in Python is a built-in function that generates a sequence of numbers. It's often used in `for` loops to repeat an action a certain number of times. The structure of the **range()** function can take one, two, or three parameters:

1. **range(n)**: This creates a sequence of numbers from **0** to **n-1**.
2. **range(start, stop)**: This creates a sequence of numbers from **start** to **stop-1**.
3. **range(start, stop, step)**: This creates a sequence of numbers from **start** to **stop-1**, incrementing by **step**.

In the line `range(i + 1, n)`, you're using the two-parameter version of **range()**. <u>It is highly recommended that you try working this `has duplicate birthday` function example out on paper or a whiteboard before reading more.</u> First, try solving it with your own technique, then try to recreate the results of the `for` loops with the `range()` function being used twice. The results should look something like this if there are 5 students indexed starting at 0 (Student #1 at index 0, Student #2 at index 1, Student #3 at index 2, etc.):

Loop 1:

    Student i is: 0 (technically student #1 but index is 0)

    ... and is being compared to

    Student j which is: 1 (Student #2 with index 1)

Loop 2:

    Student i is: 0

    ... and is being compared to

    Student j which is: 2

Loop 3:

    Student i is: 0

    ... and is being compared to

    Student j which is: 3

Loop 4:

    Student i is: 0

    ... and is being compared to

    Student j which is: 4 (technically student #5 but index is 4)

Loop 5:

    Student i is: 1

    ... and is being compared to

    Student j which is: 2

Loop 6:

    Student i is: 1

    ... and is being compared to

    Student j which is: 3

Loop 7:

    Student i is: 1

    ... and is being compared to

    Student j which is: 4

Loop 8:

    Student i is: 2

    ... and is being compared to

    Student j which is: 3

Loop 9:

    Student i is: 2

    ... and is being compared to

    Student j which is: 4

Loop 10:

    Student i is: 3

    ... and is being compared to

    Student j which is: 4

I'm sure you noticed how repetitive this process is for even a couple of students, an entire class of 30 would take 435 loops.

The time complexity of this function would be described as $O(n^2)$ because, for each student, it compares their birthday with the birthdays of all other students.

This time complexity $O(n^2)$ represents the worst-case time complexity scenario for this algorithm with n inputs. The best-case scenario would be finding a matching birthday on the first two students you compare, but the probability of that is low.

$O(n^2)$ does **not** mean that the code will always execute n^2 times. When we say an algorithm has a time complexity of $O(n^2)$, we're saying that in the worst-case scenario, the time the algorithm takes will grow quadratically with the size of the input. It's about how the runtime grows with larger inputs, rather than the exact number of operations.

This code involves two nested loops, and this is a common example of an $O(n^2)$ algorithm. However, because the inner loop doesn't always iterate from 1 to n (it iterates from i + 1 to n), the total number of iterations is not n^2 but rather an arithmetic series, and there's a formula to find the sum of such a series, in this case, it's n*(n-1)/2, equal to 10 when n is 5. Don't worry about learning arithmetic series for most coding interviews, but it would be important for at least one class for a college degree in Computer Science, I just want to explain this for clarity. In Big O notation, we usually drop constants and lower-order terms because they don't significantly impact the rate of growth for larger inputs. For this reason, $O(n^2)$ is still a suitable description for the time complexity of this algorithm.

This function is an example of quadratic time complexity, often associated with brute force solutions. **It's important to recognize that in the context of interviews and professional software engineering, such approaches are typically discouraged.** Quadratic time complexity can lead to significant performance issues, especially with large data sets. This means quadratic solutions will cost you and any company more time and money than a faster solution. Therefore, striving for more efficient solutions, such as those with constant, linear, or logarithmic time complexity, is a key skill in the field of computer science and software engineering.

Big-O Notation Summary

Understanding these different Big-O notations will help you choose the right algorithm for your task, but it depends on how much data you need to handle. Always remember: as programmers, our goal is to make software that runs efficiently and quickly, even when dealing with large amounts of data. In upcoming sections, we'll explore how different algorithms and data structures relate to these concepts.

These are just a few examples of Big-O notation. There are many other types, each representing a different relationship between the size of the input and the time or space the algorithm requires. Understanding these will help you design efficient algorithms and make better decisions in your programming journey.

A Big-O Real-world Scenario

In real-world applications, the difference between O(1) and O(log n) can be significant, especially when dealing with large data sets.

Let's consider a real-world scenario involving a database of users for a popular social media platform. Suppose this platform has billions of users and you are tasked with automating the retrieval of a specific user's profile when they log in.

If you were to use an algorithm with a time complexity of O(log n) to find a user's profile, the algorithm might involve dividing the database in half repeatedly until you locate the user. This is basically a binary search algorithm where you keep dividing a sorted list in half until you find the desired element. While this may be more efficient than searching through each user one by one (which would be O(n)), this

O(log n) solution can still be time-consuming when dealing with billions of users and **could result in web pages loading slower.**

Alternatively, if you have a function to directly access the user's profile in constant time complexity, denoted as O(1), this would be much more efficient. To implement this, each user would have a unique ID, and you have a data structure like a Python dictionary (often just called a dict) that can take that ID and instantly give you the user's profile, this would be an example of an O(1) operation. The key advantage is you're not impacted by how many users there are in the database; it takes the same small amount of time no matter what.

A Big-O Interview Question

Let's put it in a LeetCode.com problem context that may be asked during an interview. Consider a problem where you need to implement a data structure that supports insert, delete, and `get_random()` element operations, all of which should be done in O(1) time. Here, using a data structure like a list won't be efficient as a deletion in a list takes O(n) time by searching with a `for` loop. Instead, using a combination of a list (to hold the elements) and a dictionary (to hold the positions of the elements) would allow all operations to be done in O(1) time. This is a clever use of data structures that achieves constant time complexity. The related Leetcode.com problem is called "380. Insert Delete GetRandom O(1)" and you should practice it here: https://leetcode.com/problems/insert-delete-getrandom-o1/

Comparing Big-O Time Complexities using Graphs

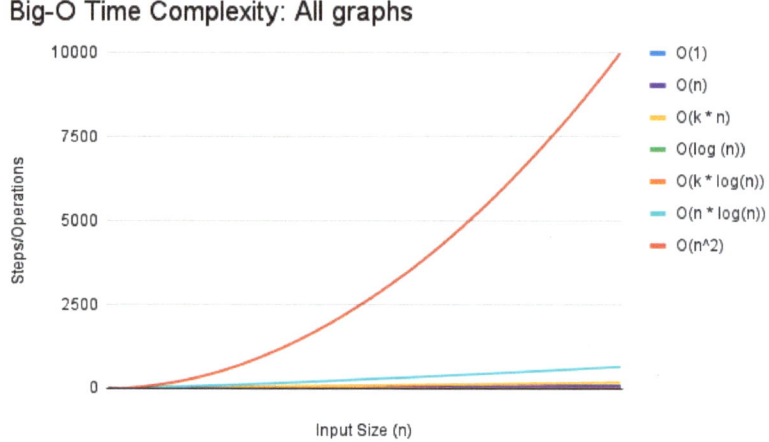

The Input Size (x-axis) is graphed from n=0 to n=100

In the above graph, $O(n^2)$ represents the slowest time complexity and appears as the highest line in red. The other complexity classes— $O(1)$, $O(\log n)$, and $O(n)$ — largely overlap and remain much lower on the scale. This stark difference illustrates the significantly slower performance associated with $O(n^2)$. In the next graphs, we will remove $O(n^2)$ to show a scale that allows us to compare the others more clearly without overlapping. As the size of the input (n) for $O(n^2)$ increases, **the number of operations or steps required by the algorithm skyrockets**. This sharp increase signifies that the time it takes for the algorithm to execute grows dramatically as the input size expands. Therefore, an algorithm with an $O(n^2)$ time complexity may become highly inefficient and time-consuming for larger inputs, <u>this will cost you or any company a lot of extra time and money so this is an important concept to remember.</u> In other words, interviewers will not like $O(n^2)$ solutions, but it's ok to start solving any problem with an $O(n^2)$ solution (also known as a brute force solution), but if you can skip to an $O(n \log n)$ solution, that's even better.

Note: Please pay attention to the different color mappings used in these graphs. The algorithm with the slowest speed is marked in red. This visual cue is intended to highlight the significant impact that time complexity can have on the efficiency of an algorithm. Remember, in the context of algorithms, **slower does not mean better!**

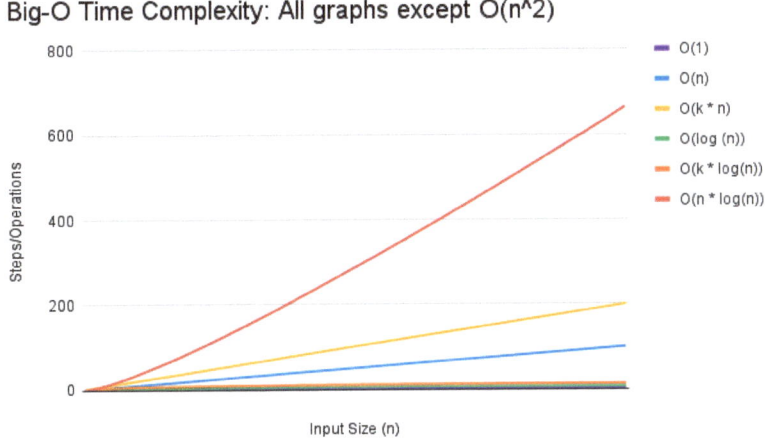

In the graph above, after removing the $O(n^2)$ graph, you'll notice that the slowest big-O time complexity is now $O(n * \log n)$. Yet still $O(1)$, $O(\log n)$, and $O(k*\log n)$ are overlapping, so those will be illustrated below.

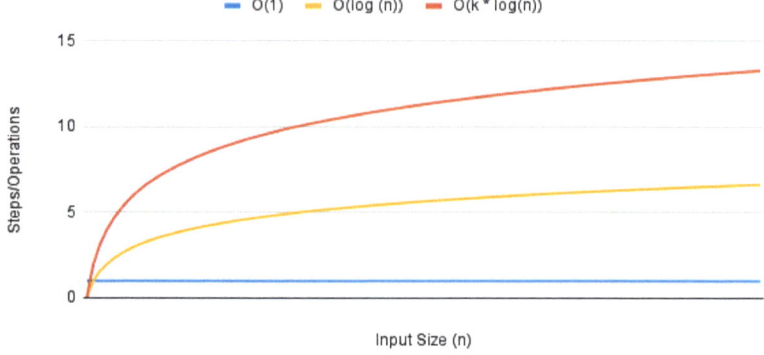

Important note: Every single graph in this chapter depicts the range of Input Size (n) from n = 0 through to n = 100.

II

Engaging Stories, Code, and Interview Solutions

In Part 2, we dive deeper into the fascinating world of coding interview problems. Here, we present a diverse collection of coding challenges and their solutions, interspersed with engaging stories that make the learning process relatable, enjoyable, and easier to remember. The stories, set in a variety of contexts, provide a unique backdrop to each problem, helping to illustrate the real-world relevance of the coding concepts being discussed.

Chapter 8

The Exclusive Music Festival

In the vibrant city of Numeralia, a highly anticipated music festival called "SoundBytes" is held every year. People from all around the world want to attend this exclusive event. Each person is given a unique QR code ticket which maps to a number, like a credit card, which grants them access to the festival. However, rumors have spread that someone has managed to duplicate a QR code, attempting to steal another person's ticket for the festival.

As people line up to enter the festival grounds, a vigilant gatekeeper function is tasked with identifying any duplicate numbers. He employs a simple, yet effective strategy. As each person approaches, he asks them to scan their QR code on a special scanner device. The device, much like a 'set' in Python, only accepts unique QR codes. If a QR code is detected to be identical to one that is already scanned, the device refuses to accept it, identifying the duplicate and preventing the counterfeiter from entering.

More specifically, if the number of scanned QR codes is equal to the number of guests that went through the line, then everyone has a unique QR code and there is no duplicate QR code. If not, there is at least one duplicate QR code.

Code Solution:

```python
class Gatekeeper:
    def containsDuplicateQR(self, guests: List[int]) -> bool:
        scanner = set(guests)
        return len(guests) != len(scanner)
```

Code Explanation:

In our Python solution, we are creating a gatekeeper function, `containsDuplicateQR`, which receives a list of 'guests'. Each 'guest' in this list is represented by a number, and we're looking for duplicates.

Here are two input/output examples:

Example 1:

   Input: nums = [2, 3, 2]

   Output: True

Example 2:

   Input: nums = [1, 2, 3, 5]

   Output: False

We create a 'set' from this list, which we call 'scanner'. A set in Python is a data structure that only allows unique elements - much like our story. If we try to add a duplicate element to a set, it simply won't be added and the set length won't change.

Then, we compare the length of the original list of 'guests' with the length of the 'scanner'. If there's a duplicate in the 'guests' list, the length of 'scanner' will be less than the length of 'guests', because the set didn't add the duplicate elements. If there are no duplicates, the lengths will be equal, as every 'guest' had a unique QR code to scan on the device and this function would return 'False'. This function returns 'True' if there is at least one duplicate QR code in the line.

The time complexity of this solution is O(n), where n is the number of guests. This is because creating a set from a list in Python iterates over the list once, so the time complexity is linear with respect to the size of the input.

The space complexity of this solution is also O(n), where n is the number of guests. This is because a set is a data structure that stores unique elements from the list. The worst-case time complexity occurs when all guests have unique QR codes and the 'scanner' set will have the same number of elements as the 'guests' list. To be clear, the worst-case time complexity happening would be a good thing because that means nobody tried to steal a ticket. Therefore, the space complexity is proportional to the size of the input.

In summary, this Python solution is very efficient, with both time and space complexity of O(n).

This problem is inspired by the Leetcode.com problem called "217. Contains Duplicate" and you should practice it here:

https://leetcode.com/problems/contains-duplicate/

Enjoyed this book?

If you liked reading this book, check out Cracking Python Volume 2 on Amazon! Volume 2 will have 9 more stories like "The Exclusive Music Festival".

About the Author

Halin Garcia-Gordon stands at the forefront of the technology industry, with a career marked by collaborations with Cisco and other top-tier tech giants, he has over a decade of experience in propelling digital innovations through software engineering and cybersecurity innovation. Halin's expertise extends to academia, where he is currently in a Cybersecurity Graduate Program at Stanford University, pursuing credit toward his Master's in Computer Science at Stanford University. He also graduated with a Bachelor of Science in Software Engineering from San Jose State University. He currently serves as the CEO and Founder of Datasophical, a San Jose, California-based company specializing in writing and publishing educational e-books that teach coding and business skills. Datasophical also provides Wi-Fi support to businesses. His record of enhancing customer experiences, such as improving the payment system Wi-Fi at various San Francisco Bay Area businesses demonstrates his commitment to excellence.

His impressive career trajectory includes managing the Security Operations Development team at Cisco Meraki as a Security Development Manager and leading the F5 Trust team as the Lead AWS Security Engineer. From automating security operations using Python to managing over 20 AWS cloud accounts, Halin's prowess in cybersecurity and software engineering is unmistakable.

In addition to his remarkable professional and academic accomplishments, Halin is an accomplished pianist with a love for jazz and classical music. His renditions of pieces such as Chopin's Revolutionary Etude Op. 10 No. 12 and John Legend's "Ordinary People" can be found on YouTube.

But Halin's passion extends beyond his work and music. He is a passionate mentor, dedicated to helping the next generation of engineers and entrepreneurs. He has volunteered his time with organizations like The Hidden Genius Project and CODE2040, and his diverse team of high school students and tech professionals even won first place at President Obama's My Brother's Keeper Hackathon organized by Qeyno Labs.

Halin Garcia-Gordon, with his extensive expertise, profound understanding, and fervent dedication to mentorship, is at the forefront of software engineering innovation. His unwavering pursuit of excellence and empowerment has paved the way for significant advancements in the field. A guide, a mentor, and a trailblazer, Halin does more than just navigate the terrain of technological progress—he shapes it. As you journey through his work, prepare to be inspired and equipped with the knowledge and skills to elevate your expertise, and perhaps, reshape the future of technology yourself.

You can connect with me on:

- https://github.com/Datasophical/CrackingPythonVol1
- https://www.linkedin.com/in/halin